KIDS CAN HELP

A First Look

KATIE PETERS

GRL Consultant, Diane Craig, Certified Literacy Specialist

Lerner Publications ◆ Minneapolis

Educator Toolbox

Reading books is a great way for kids to express what they're interested in. Before reading this title, ask the reader these questions:

What do you think this book is about? Look at the cover for clues.

What do you already know about helping others?

What do you want to learn about helping others?

Let's Read Together

Encourage the reader to use the pictures to understand the text.

Point out when the reader successfully sounds out a word.

Praise the reader for recognizing sight words such as *can* and *the*.

TABLE OF CONTENTS

Kids Can Help 4

Kids Can Help

I like to help people
around me.
There are many ways
I can help!

I give away toys and clothes I don't need.

Other kids can
enjoy them.

Some people don't have homes.
I go with my family to help serve them meals.

I get food to give away.
It will go to people who
are hungry.

Where could you pick up trash?

I pick up trash in the park.

I help plant a
garden to share.

What would you
grow in a garden?

I visit people in
a nursing home.

We read together.

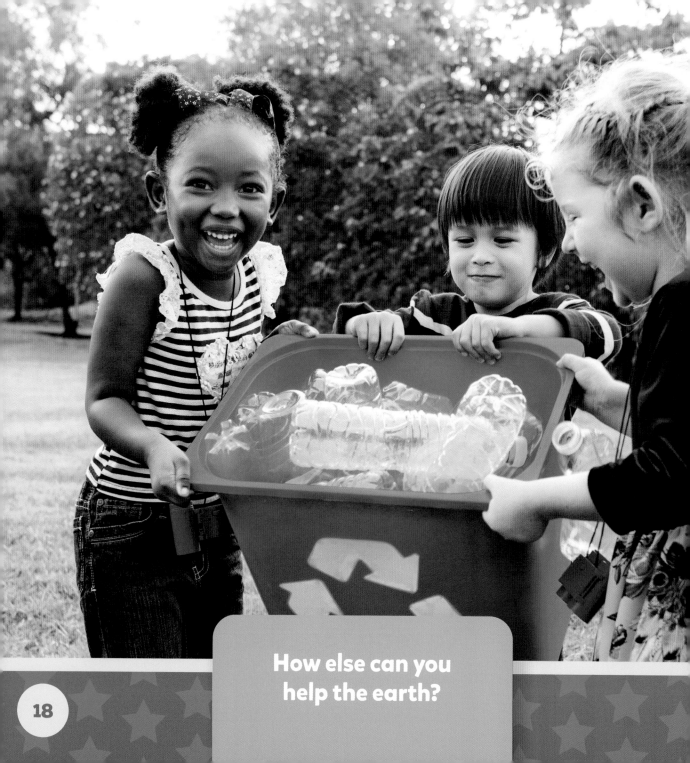

How else can you
help the earth?

I help the earth.
I put cans, bottles,
and paper in the
blue bin.

Helping feels good!

You Connect!

What other ways can you think of to help others?

What is something fun you do to help others?

What is something new you would like to do to help others?

Social and Emotional Snapshot

Student voice is crucial to building reader confidence. Ask the reader:

What is your favorite part of this book?

What is something you learned from this book?

Did this book remind you of any ways you have helped out?

Photo Glossary

bottles

garden

nursing home

trash

Learn More

Lindeen, Mary. *Reduce, Reuse, and Recycle, Oscar!* Minneapolis: Lerner Publications, 2020.

Murray, Julie. *Citizenship.* Minneapolis: Abdo, 2020.

Rossiter, Brienna. *Volunteering.* Lake Elmo, MN: Focus Readers, 2021.

Index

Photo Acknowledgments

The images in this book are used with the permission of: © lovelyday12/Shutterstock Images, pp. 4–5; © Pixel-Shot/Shutterstock Images, p. 6; © Symchych Maria/Adobe Stock, p. 7; © Gorodenkoff/Shutterstock Images, pp. 8–9; © deryabinka/Shutterstock Images, p. 10; © Nicholas F/peopleimages.com/Adobe Stock, pp. 10–11; © narikan/Shutterstock Images, pp. 12–13, 23; © Quality Stock Arts/Adobe Stock, p. 14; © Maria Sbytova/Adobe Stock, pp. 14–15, 23; © WavebreakMediaMicro/Adobe Stock, pp. 16, 23; © KARNSTOCKS/Shutterstock Images, p. 17; © Rawpixel.com/Shutterstock Images, pp. 18–19, 23; © Tapui/Shutterstock Images, p. 20.

Cover Photograph: © .Pixel-Shot/Adobe Stock

Design Elements: © Mighty Media, Inc.

Lerner Publications Company
An imprint of Lerner Publishing Group, Inc.
241 First Avenue North
Minneapolis, MN 55401 USA

For reading levels and more information, look up this title at www.lernerbooks.com.

Main body text set in Mikado a Medium.
Typeface provided by Hannes von Doehren.

Library of Congress Cataloging-in-Publication Data

Names: Peters, Katie, author.
Title: Kids can help : a first look / Katie Peters, GRL Consultant, Diane Craig, Certified Literacy Specialist.
Description: Minneapolis : Lerner Publications, [2024] | Series: Read about citizenship (read for a better world) | Includes bibliographical references and index. | Audience: Ages 5–8 | Audience: Grades K–1 | Summary: "It feels good to help people in need. Leveled text and full-color photographs show readers what they can do to help others in their community"—Provided by publisher.
Identifiers: LCCN 2023010627 (print) | LCCN 2023010628 (ebook) | ISBN 9798765608753 (library binding) | ISBN 9798765624609 (paperback) | ISBN 9798765616505 (epub)
Subjects: LCSH: Helping behavior in children—Juvenile literature. | Helping behavior—Juvenile literature.
Classification: LCC BF723.H45 P48 2024 (print) | LCC BF723.H45 (ebook) | DDC 155.4/182–dc23/eng/20230616

LC record available at https://lccn.loc.gov/2023010627
LC ebook record available at https://lccn.loc.gov/2023010628

Manufactured in the United States of America
1 – CG – 12/15/23